Bibliographic information published by the German National Library:

The German National Library lists this publication in the National Bibliography; detailed bibliographic data are available on the Internet at http://dnb.dnb.de .

Imprint:

Copyright © 2016 GRIN Verlag, Open Publishing GmbH
Print and binding: Books on Demand GmbH, Norderstedt Germany
ISBN: 9783668261143

This book at GRIN:

http://www.grin.com/en/e-book/322415/information-systems-and-decision-support-systems

Ioannis Panges

Information Systems and Decision Support Systems

GRIN Publishing

GRIN - Your knowledge has value

Since its foundation in 1998, GRIN has specialized in publishing academic texts by students, college teachers and other academics as e-book and printed book. The website www.grin.com is an ideal platform for presenting term papers, final papers, scientific essays, dissertations and specialist books.

Visit us on the internet:

http://www.grin.com/

http://www.facebook.com/grincom

http://www.twitter.com/grin_com

Information Systems and Decision Support Systems

This text was written by a non-native English speaker. Please excuse any errors or inconsistencies.

Summary

Information Systems developed to help users to achieve their goals. If we look at international level, the introduction of information technology and general information systems in everyday life, we will see that this admission has been made successfully by-produces the expected results in countries characterized by good organization of public life other, individual systems, banking system, health system, are well organized and staffed.

On the other hand, Decision Support Systems represent a combined approach of decision making from the Administration area with tools and IT techniques. A widely accepted definition describes the DSS as computer software which accepts as input data a large number of events and methods to convert comparisons, graphs and directions in some sense, that facilitate and expand the capabilities of what takes decisions.

Keywords: Information Systems, Information Systems Decision Making

1. What are Information Systems
1.1. Definitions

Information (Information) is any form of communication, which provides comprehensive and money-level- knowledge to the person who takes it. In other words, the information is data that are structured to be easily understandable and useful to people. Data are the raw material of each IT system and form the basis for the setting-miourgia information [11].

As a **system** can be defined a number of related elements which perform an activity, function or task. The systems are divided into open and closed. Open called the systems affected by the environment (or affect) and closed called those not affected by the environment, nor the influence. The information systems are open systems because process information from their environment, not process the information available to them [12].

The open and closed systems differ in their entropy. Entropy is the concept by which you measure the **"disorder"**, whose maximum value reflects the total disarray and is equivalent to the termination of life or otherwise of evolution [9]. In open systems, the "order" and therefore its entropy remains constant, increases or decreases depending on the input (input) of the maintenance. In closed systems, the entropy never reduced because they are not maintenance input. In the area of information systems, the term open system mainly refers to those systems that Bo-Rooney to work with software (software), and equipment (hardware) from various procure-ers, and the term closed to those which can operate software and equipmention from a single supplier. It is understood that the open systems are more flexible and the current trend is the dynamic movement from closed to open systems.

Information systems called a set of procedures, human resources and computer systems for collecting, recording, per-acquisition, processing, storage and analysis. These systems may include software, hardware and telecommunications arm [12].

Information systems are the means for the harmonious cooperation human dynamic, data, processes and information and communication technologies.They emerged as a bridge between the practical applications of computer science and business.

Any special information system is aimed at business support, management and decision making. In a broad sense, the term is used to refer not only to the information and communication technology (ICT), an organization use-it employs, but the way in which people interact with this technology to support business processes.

Therefore, the computer systems associated with the data annealed base management systems on the one hand and the business systems on the other. An information system is a system of communication format in which data is represented and treated as a form of social memory. An information system may also be considered as a semi-formal language which supports downloads from human-phase and action [10].

1.2. Components of an Information System

In order for someone to understand the information systems should understand the problem to solve their architectural and design elements and procedure-vices in the body that lead to these solutions. The term Information Systems is-shall be the following: People, Data, Information Technology, Hardware, Processes.

People consist of roles either Users (End Users, managers, owner recommended-it), operators Creators (Developers, analysts, database designer, network specialist, manager project)

Data-Procedures processed by PS They depend on the nature of the organization and the user requirements. Procedures are instructions for people belonging to PS Depending on the type of system state changes and the complexity of procedure-vices.

Technologies Informatics include:

- The system (operation system)
- The Applications (library, accounting, payroll)
- The Productivity (NW management tools, fourth generation languages and CASE tools, word processors).

1.2.1. The basic components of a Computer Information System

One Computer Information System essentially uses the Computation-Maximum technology to perform some or all of the scheduled tasks. The main co-static computer-based information system:

- Hardware - these are the devices such as the display, processor, printer and keyboard, which cooperate to receive.
- Software - are programs that allow the material to process the data.
- Databases - is the concentration of related files or tables Flex IP-related data.
- Networks - is a coupling system that allows several computers to at-allocation of resources.
- Procedures - are the commands for the combination of the above components, to processing-down information, and to produce the preferred output [3].

2. What decision

Decision is choosing between two or more alternatives. According to this definition, the decision making is the process of selecting between two or more lactones alternator solutions. The need for the selection results from the distance between a current and a desired condition. The many options refer to ways in which the existing situation will be brought to the desired or undesired condition.

The M. Simon gives a more complete definition of decision-making. It argues that the decision making is a process which consists in finding opportunities for making a decision (current desired-state difference) to find possible courses of action (alternatives) and the choice between modes of action (decision) [9].

The stages for the decision-making process are the following:

- Determination of the problem / opportunity
- Identification of alternatives
- Analysis and evaluation of alternatives
- Select the best solution
- Implementation of the program
- Evaluation of the program

2.1. What is a Decision Support System (DSS)

As Decision Support System (DSS) is defined as an information system contend radicals taking semistructured and unstructured decisions, which can not be described algorithmically in the data and the processes required to obtain them. A DSS has the following characteristics:
• Assists decision-makers (but not replace) "by extending their capabilities» (extending their capabilities), namely:

- speeding up data
- accelerating data processing
- reinforcing conclusions
- enhancing memory that decides
- enhancing the knowledge of this taking the decision (eg by providing access to relevant knowledge others) [6].

2.1.1. Structure of a Decision Support System (DSS)

The main structure of these systems consists of a knowledge base, a mechanism universe-sion, illustrating a camera and a communication module with the user. The knowledge base is the most important component, since it contains all the relevant knowledge.

The explanation Engine allows the user to check the correctness of the reasoning which led to the solutions by providing analysis of logical relationships that lead to the before-enon solution.

The conclusions Mechanism, is able to combine the knowledge base data to synthesize the optimal solution. When communicating with the user of these systems, U-povalloun user a set of questions to gather information Anal--financed, so the conclusions mechanism uses the input data looking at knowledge base the knowledge on which will create more than an appropriate advice.

The user interface is a method in which using questions - answers or data from other systems, the user has available the appropriate advice accompanied by an analysis of the steps that led to it [21].

2.2. Decision Support System Structure (DSS)

As the E. Loukis, (2010) a DSS is usually a system of integrated IT-mind the Enterprise System. The MIS includes additionally a series dispatcher's subsystems (operational subsystems), each of which SUPPORT-live the completion of an operation (or part of an operation) of the enterprise.

The components of a decision support subsystem, besides the data warehouse are as follows:

✓ On-line Analytical Processing Tools (analytical processing tools)
✓ Data Mining Tools (data mining tools)
✓ Decision Modeling Tools - Effectiveness Modeling Tools (decision problems Modeling Tools - effectiveness)
✓ User Modeling Tools (User Modeling Tools)

3. The Decision Support System features

The studies make that a decision support system is able to improve the epi-firm helping with the automatic provision of decision support as part of the flow of daily operations, supporting decisions in space and time of the AU-of making incitement to action beyond simple assessment of the facts and the electronic use computer systems.

Time is an important feature in the service environment, so a decision support In-system ensures that it saves time, without introducing undesirable-neither delays nor increases the workload for managers, as it requires minimum time operation in [7].

Decision support systems are urging the user to preventive actions et-so easy to escape the attention in the effort to address the immediate problem of program-product or service.

The response speed of these systems, a criterion of success and adoption on the part of the professionals providing high quality of services and reduce costs for their practical application.

3.1. Applications of Decision Support
3.1.1. Historical evolution

The area of Decision Support Systems also has a variety of applications for the needs of the agencies after the first 70s widely used approaches. Part of these applications generally approaches the problem of decision-making, either through alternative theoretical approaches, or using different technology. Al-if developed with a view to their application to specific problems and environment-da job. Then, a brief reference to the different type of applications that were developed during the last thirty years.

The most important development in the field of suffer-rupture Decision Systems was the transition from systems supporting decision making by an individual user, in systems that allow the communication and cooperation of a user group [15,16,22]. In particular, reported the Information Systems Corporate Executives (Executive Information Systems - EIS) which provided support to managers of enterprises, the Support Systems Group Decision (Group Decision Support Systems-GDSS) and Operational Support Systems De-phase (Organizational Decision Support Systems-ODSS).

The Internet-based Decision Support Systems (Web-based Decision Support Systems) were a novelty during the 90s, allowing access to different types of information sources and online collaboration of decision makers [14,13,19, 20]. These applications were based on the development of four new tools, Data Warehouse (Data Warehouses), modern analytical puri--processing (on-line analytical processing-OLAP), data mining (data mining) and the Global Reporting Web (World Wide Web). The use of these tools allowed the development of more efficient, flexible, friendly to use and powerful computing systems-bleed. On the other hand, the development of a system became more complex, and as a major issue highlighted the compatibility of new applications with the past and their maintenance costs.

From a technological perspective, the future of the DSS will be further enriched with tools and next generation services (mobile e-services) and applied-wireless access tions (eg Wireless Applications Protocol-WAP, Wireless Markup Lan-guage - WML), allowing in this way a more sophisticated, flexible and easy-importance of access to information and decision support tools. On the other hand, as already mentioned, the strengthening of the Decision Support Systems with techniques and tools of Knowledge Management System is considered as the most promising developments

3.1.2. Comparative Endorsement Decision Support Systems

With the ultimate aim of developing a Base Model which will make multi-criteria analysis to classify a series of discrete alternatives. The SELECT-earth presentation of methods of multicriteria analysis stems from the fact that TE-TolC kind of methods have been widely used in group decision-making environments. The widespread use because they provide solutions to poorly structured problems, allowing the group decision makers to take into account a number of criteria and a set of alternatives. Also, these methods provide the possibility of recovery-dure of alternatives both quantitative and qualitative criteria.

For these reasons, and with a view to establishing a set of rules for choosing the most appropriate method depending on the problem to be solved, in Paros-like phase will be presented to solve a strategic problem. The aim of resolving this problem with systems based on four of the most classical to-Methods multicriteria analysis is the comparison of these visa. The results of a TE-toias comparison can help to develop rules which would allow a decision-maker to choose the most appropriate method for the purpose of to solve the problem based on existing data and the desired effect [17].

3.2. Factors affecting the inapplicability

The integration of decision support systems in everyday practice is relatively limited due to the specificity of each sector enterprise where data, fa-out in narrative form or not, which makes the expression and their representation in the knowledge base, complex. The information and data specified by tissue and characteristics of each case, increasing the complexity of decisions.

The key factor in the implementation of these systems is the human resources of company sometimes remains negatively disposed to the use of these tools, believing that it can replace them. It has been observed that the unwieldy user interfaces, preventing staff from using them, but in fact is a handy tool that helps solve many everyday problems and avoid business errors [18].

4. Conclusions

The adoption of decision support systems in everyday business practice help to avoid errors and to increase the level of provided service-vices [6].It is a particular interest in the IT field, involving the coordinated work of all stakeholders based integrated project, which will take into account the experiences and current technological developments.

The full introduction of these systems facilitate user access to the functionality provided by the use of a computer or a smart mobile phone device, which is covered and the requirement for increased mobility has been an employee in the decision-making systems. According to some researchers the systems support systems constitute a single strategy that takes advantage of the experience, knowledge, current technological developments in other European countries [23.1].

In this effort, the employees of the firm involved in all stages of the life cycle devel-opment of these systems (design, development, use, extension), employed poiontas modern knowledge representation standards that allow the use of knowledge by reducing the cost and time.

Bibliographical references
Greek
1. A. Vagelatos, I. Sarivougioukas (2005). Success factors for the introduction of information systems in hospitals. Inspection of Health 24-29

2. K. Gialelis, D. Demetriades, Ch. Kalergis, A. Chestnut et al (2010) .Efarmoges Software. OAED Publications, Athens.

3. Giannakopoulos, D., Papoutsis, I. (2003). Management Information Systems. Co-stroke Publications, Athens.

4. B. Dranidis, (2004). Information Systems, Computer Science Notes STEF - Information Systems. Chameleon

5. SE Katsanou (1993) .Fysikochimeia. Papazisis, Athens.

6. C. Kolostoumpis, K. Makrigiannakis, A. Christodoulos (2010). Health Information System-automatically: Evaluation Criteria for Existing & Future situation. 8th National Conference of Public Health & Health Services, pp. 182

7. A. Lazakidou (2005). Hospital Information Systems & Electronic ser- vices-Health, Athens.

8. MC Lucia (2010). Decision Support Systems. Aegean University

9. D. Bourandas, N. Papalexandri (1998). Introduction to business administration. Publishers-ye Benos, Athens.

10. SG Economou, VN (Georgopoulos, 1995) .Pliroforiaka systems for business administration. Administration information system. Publications E. Benos, Athens.

11. C. Economou, N. Georgopoulos (1995). Information Systems Management E-picheiriseon. Publications E. Benos, Athens.

12. D. Folinas (2006). "Integrated information argument vegetables-resource management systems." Publications Anikoula, Athens

English
13. Bhargava, H. and D. J. Power (2001). Decision Support Systems and Web Technologies: A Status Report. Proceedings of the 2001 Americas Conference on Information Systems, Boston.

14. Dhar V. Stein R (1997). Intelligent decision support methods. Prentice Hall

15. J.A. Gray (1981). A critique of Eysenck's theory of personality, In H.J. Eysenck (Ed.) A model for personality.

16. J. Huber, J.W. Payne, C. Puto (1982). Adding Assymetrically Dominated Alternatives: Violations of Regularity and the Similarity Hypothesis. The Journal of Consumer Re-search, Vol.9, pp. 90-98.

17. Poole, M.S., Holmes, M., Watson, R. and DeSanctis, G. (1993). Group decision support systems and group communication. Communication Research, Vol. 20, pp. 133-145.

18. D.J. Power (2000). Web-based and model-driven decision support systems: Concepts and issues. In Proceedings of: The 2000 Americas Conference on Information Systems, Long Beach, California.

19. D. J. Power (2002). Decision Support Systems: Concepts and Resources for Managers, Westport, CT: Greenwood / Quorum.

20. T. C. Powell, (2001). Competitive advantage: logical and philosophical considerations. Strat. Mgmt. J., 22: 875-888.

21. Stephens, W. and Middleton, T. (2002). Why has the uptake of Decision Support Systems been so poor? In: Crop-soil simulation models in developing countries. Wallingford: CABI.

22. M. Turoff, Hiltz, S. R. (1982). The electronic journal: A progress report. Journal of the American Society for Information Science, 33 (4), 195-202.

23. A. Wright, Sitting DF, JS Ash, S. Sharma, J.E Pang, Middleton B (2009). Clinical decision support capabilities of commercially-available clinical information systems, JAM Med Inform Assoc., Vol 16.

YOUR KNOWLEDGE HAS VALUE